showhouses

JEFFREY B. SNYDER

JEFFREY B. SNYDER

show houses 3

A DECORATORS' TOUR

Schiffer Publishing Ltd

4880 Lower Valley Road • Atglen, PA 19310

Other Schiffer Books by the Author:
Art Glass Today. ISBN: 978-0-7643-3464-1. $50.00
Asian Ivory. ISBN: 978-0-7643-2728-5. $79.95
Canes & Walking Sticks: A Stroll Through Time and Place. ISBN: 0-7643-2041-6. $69.95
Ceramics Today. ISBN: 978-0-7643-3465-8. $50.00
Mosaic Art Today. ISBN: 978-0-7643-4001-7. $50.00
Printmakers Today. ISBN: 978-0-7643-3462-7. $50.00
Rookwood Pottery. ISBN: 0-7643-2277-X. $89.95
Showhouses 2: A Decorators' Tour. ISBN: 978-0-7643-3649-2. $45.00

Other Schiffer Books on Related Subjects:
Decorator Show Houses. Tina Skinner, Melissa Cardona, & Nancy Ottino. ISBN: 0-7643-2051-3. $44.95
Designer Showcase: Interior Design at its Best. Melissa Cardona and Nathaniel Wolfgang-Price. ISBN: 0-7643-2398-9. $44.95
Showhouse Review: An Exposé of Interior Decorating Events. Tina Skinner. ISBN: 978-0-7643-2864-0. $44.95
Showhouses 1: A Decorators' Tour. Tina Skinner. ISBN: 978-0-7643-3272-2. $44.99

Published by Schiffer Publishing, Ltd.
4880 Lower Valley Road
Atglen, PA 19310
Phone: (610) 593-1777; Fax: (610) 593-2002
E-mail: Info@schifferbooks.com

For the largest selection of fine reference books on this and related subjects, please visit our website at **www.schifferbooks.com**. You may also write for a free catalog.

This book may be purchased from the publisher.
Please try your bookstore first.

We are always looking for people to write books on new and related subjects. If you have an idea for a book, please contact us at **proposals@schifferbooks.com**

Schiffer Books are available at special discounts for bulk purchases for sales promotions or premiums. Special editions, including personalized covers, corporate imprints, and excerpts can be created in large quantities for special needs. For more information contact the publisher.

In Europe, Schiffer books are distributed by:
Bushwood Books
6 Marksbury Ave.
Kew Gardens
Surrey TW9 4JF England
Phone: 44 (0) 20 8392 8585; Fax: 44 (0) 20 8392 9876
E-mail: info@bushwoodbooks.co.uk
Website: www.bushwoodbooks.co.uk

Designed by RoS
Bodoni MT/Aldine 721 BT

ISBN: 978-0-7643-4174-8
Printed in China

Dedication

To Mike and Madeline for adding so much joy to our lives.

contents

To walk into a decorator showhouse is to enter the realm of ideas—new ideas on products, styles, and colors—fired by talented designers' inspirations, visions, and flights of fancy. Both the general public and professional designers alike receive insight walking through these amazing spaces.

Designer showhouses are open to the public, largely during the spring and early summer months of April, May, and June. However, summer and fall showhouses are found in Northern states in the United States, while February finds showhouses ready to go in balmy Florida.

Multitudes of dedicated volunteers work with designers to make magic happen within the walls of a designer showhouse. Interiors of mostly historic homes are transformed and deadlines met to create the impression of serene and seamless beauty with no hint of the mad scramble of design and fabrication that occurred before the doors swung smoothly open on the first day. For weeks, crowds come and viewers are inspired and amazed by the transformations found in each and every room. Once the doors close for the final time, the interiors of the venerable home are returned to their former state, donations are made to worthy hospitals and charities, and the show is done.

introd

Showhouses are ephemeral creatures. Captured here are the designs that came and went from a variety of showhouses from near the end of the first and the beginning of the second decades of the twenty-first century. Those transient masterpieces of interior design are preserved for all those who could not attend the original shows. The venue has changed, but the inspiration remains the same. So open the door and tour these transformed historical homes room by room, all by yourself ... or bring a friend along. There is always room for one more.

uction

foyers&

hallways

Interlude
2010 RNS Showhouse at the Shore, Ocean City, New Jersey
Betsy King of Jupiter Dunes Designs
Photography by: John Armich

In this 1907 Dutch Colonial home, "Windsong on Wesley," the main stairway may be seen from the living room at the base of the steps and the four bedrooms along the top landing. It is an interlude between two worlds. The entire area was painted a pale green, with the walls accented with three long, narrow glass and metallic leaf contemporary sea-siren paintings by Suzanne Reese Horvitz. A cozy multi-fabric upholstered built-in bench is under the small window on the first landing. I designed and fabricated a pierced copper inset panel in the back of the bench. Under the bench, antiqued-finished copper storage drawers with brushed steel accents contrast with the pale green organza and glass bead window treatment above the bench. A recycled steel and green glass chandelier by Varaluz was chosen that gives the feel of a canopy of bubbles under the sea.

"Glitz and Glamour Galore" Foyer
Washington Design Center 2010 Design House, Washington, DC
Kelley Proxmire of Kelley Interior Design
Photography by: Greg Powers Photography

Envisioned here was the Park Avenue home of a New York socialite, the backdrop for big entertaining. The inspiration for the room began with a pair of turquoise vases discovered at the Charlotte Moss Townhouse in Manhattan. Building on this defining shade of blue and a love for black and white, the room is a study in graphic contrasts and glamorous finishes.

The unexpected focal point is the floor. In lieu of a rug, the floor was painted in a David Hicks-inspired black and white octagonal pattern, a look both bold and classic. Aside from the floor, patterns in the room are restrained. The skirted table is vibrant turquoise outlined in a bold black-and-white trim. Window treatments in crisp white silk are accented with a simple trim in turquoise on the leading edges, the bottom of the panels, and on the valance. Walls are finished in a simple, yet sophisticated white grasscloth from Schumacher.

Patterns may be restrained, but the scale of the pieces in the room reads dramatic. The two console tables were originally built as dining tables; the mirrors above them soar to nearly five feet. A sweeping wall of French doors gain added impact painted black.

Accent pieces add the dazzle and refinement of jewelry to this punchy room. Crystal table lamps dispense sparkle throughout. Mirrors and wall sconces extend the luxurious gold tones. An oversized gilded chandelier by Niermann Weeks graces the center skirted table adorned with rhinestones.

Summer Nights Foyer
Cape May's Sixth Annual (2010) Designer Show House
Carole Roach of DRD & Associates
Photography by: John Armich

After a long day at the beach or a day of traveling to Cape May, the entry into this bed and breakfast is a welcome sight. The inviting foyer separated by flowing striped drapery leads you into a relaxing, old-fashioned front porch. Comfortable seating gives a perfect view of two original paintings by a local artist. The porch is a retreat for early morning coffee or late evening cocktails.

Riders' Hearthside Retreat
The 35th Bucks County Designer House and Gardens Fieldstone Farm
Kelley Price of Kelley Price Interiors
Photography by: Katrina Mojzesz of Top Kat Photography Inc.

Riders' Hearthside Retreat is an inviting, equestrian entryway to the home and a place to relax anytime of day. The space provides corner window seats for a morning cup of tea, classic leather chairs to read a book in the afternoon, and a warm velvet chaise for warming up by the fire with a glass of wine in the evening.

Aesthetically, the room is draped with luxurious fabrics on the windows, window seat, and upholstered furniture balancing the hardscape of the exquisite stone fireplace. The suede walls envelope the room. A punch of red and lime green complement the earthy brown tones. The result, a warm, welcoming first impression for your thoroughbred home.

Deux Petit Salons
Mansion in May Designer Show House, 2012, Fawn Hill Farm Estate, Morristown, New Jersey
Kenneth/Davis

The design was inspired by our stays at magnificent chateaus, villas, and castles throughout Europe and Africa, as well as the fabulous parties thrown by our friends, including Princess Thurn und Taxis. We believe that the foyer should no longer be a passage way to other rooms. It should be a useable and functional space. Here is an entry way, an entertaining area, a seating area, and a gallery for artwork on both levels. We have combined the use of contemporary with traditional elements, which also include the use of green items, such as the chandeliers and seating. To add drama, moldings were added. The entire space was lacquered gloss white and the floors darkened to increase the perception of height.

Farmhouse Entrance

Napa Valley Symphony League 2010 Home and Garden Tour, Yountville, California, An Italian Style Farmhouse
Joyce Hoshall of Joyce Hoshall, Interiors
Photography by: Dave Adams

Shown here is the stone entrance to an Italian farmhouse.

Foyer and Gallery
Baltimore Symphony Associates 2010 Decorator Show House, Pikesville, Maryland
Pat O'Brien
Photography by: John Coyle

The painted feathers floating about the foyer walls in this Tudor style home lend a light and airy feel to the space. Ornamentation is kept primarily to the walls, permitting easy movement throughout. The Tudor style evokes images of knights in shining armor, dragons, and jewels; images that are portrayed in the artwork. Follow the floating feathers up the grand, circular stairway to the gallery space above. Aspects of medieval times are visible in the artwork in this gallery space as well. Relax on the banana leaf benches to admire an art collection fit for royalty!

Entry, Powder Room, and Mezzanine
44th Pasadena Showcase House of Design
Gregory Parker of Parker West Interiors
Photography by: Alexander Vertikoff

The entry to this Spanish Revival home is grand in its simplicity and always maintains a clean line. It is wise in design work to respect the architecture of the home in which you are working. The wood coffered ceiling is original and was restored. The existing chandelier was modified. The chandelier was relocated to be more central in the room. A chandelier lift was installed to easily change out electric lighting. Function is not sacrificed for beauty. The original Batchelder fountain was also redesigned to add a strong, vertical element and makes a grand statement. The ceilings in this entry are a generous twenty-eight feet. One cannot be too sensitive to the effects of scale when working out the design details in a room. This space was designed to be used for live music, an added dimension bringing life and warmth to the house.

The original magnesite floors were restored and enhanced. It is essential to have a clear understanding of how natural light works in a room. The Spanish Revival style tends to be dark and dramatic. So, to maximize natural light, the walls are light in color. The ebonized carved mirrors also enhance the feeling of light. Since these mirrors are over seven feet tall and were hung sixteen feet up the wall, I was on pins and needles watching this installation!

Windows are intentionally left without treatment to emphasize the charming architectural detail. The distinctive Arts and Craft ceramic collection on the mezzanine underline the soft palette of cool colors with warm shadings. The spectacular antique tapestries lend an authentic air and furniture is well chosen for balance between traditional and modern sensibilities.

studies&

libraries

First Floor Study
Cape May's Fifth Annual Designer Show House
Mark D. Little of Design Home Interiors
Photography by: John Armich

The study is a serene oasis of warm wood tones against soft neutrals and gentle curves inspired by the sandy beaches of the coast.

Mountain Top Study
2008 Cashiers Designer Showhouse Study
Patricia McLean Interiors, Inc.
Photography by: Patricia McLean Interiors, Inc.

Inspired by the scenery outside, a faux artist was commissioned to custom paint screens from photos taken of the area. The colors were soft and muted and brought the room to life. The leather chair was wide and low to the ground, which helped on the scale. The daybed is antique French. The mantle was addressed with a mirror to add light. Small table serves as a book rest as the room is too small for a coffee table. The daybed is loaded with down pillows for comfort reading or napping. The draperies are a lovely green tone with gold floral sprigs that look reminiscent of the area.

The bookcase is loaded with antique jugs. The cream color brought light to the space. Library steps are wonderful end tables. A potty seat houses the price list for the room. In case you don't know, all items in the Show House rooms are for sale and a percentage goes to charity.

Artist's Study

2010 DC Design House, Chevy Chase, Maryland
Tracy Morris of Tracy Morris Design
Photography by: Angie Seckinger

A depiction of an artist's study, reflecting a sophisticated and understated montage of textures, colors, and mediums. Painted floors evoke a French farmhouse feel, while walls in cool neutral allow the palette of the featured paintings to take center stage. Textural notes continue with a Lucite desk and velvet chair. Woven and light window treatments complete the space. The room exudes a sense of calm and comfort offering the perfect environment in which to relax, think, and, most importantly, create.

Rose Hill Library/Study
Rose Hill, Wilmore, Kentucky
Joe T. Richardson, Carolyn Threlkeld, and Bobbie Alloo of Hubbuch & Co.
Photography by: Walt Roycraft

Rose Hill served as home for the president of Asbury
Seminary. The design in the library/study concentrated
on seating comfort among the many books and collections
of Majolica and antique glassware.

GlenLary Farm Library/Study
2010 Decorator Showcase, GlenLary Farm, Paris, Kentucky
Joe T. Richardson, Carolyn Threlkeld, and Bobbie Alloo of Hubbuch & Co.
Photography by: Walt Roycraft

The design of the library/study featured paneling and bookcases done in cherry wood. The faux bois treatment on the mantel and doors match the wood finish in the rest of the room. An oval desk covered entirely in leather was featured on an antique Oushak rug. Contemporary furnishings were mixed with antique accessories and books, which were complemented with comfortable upholstered seating.

"Queen of Hearts" Library/Game Room
Princeton Designer Showhouse & Gardens XVI
Totten-McGuirl Interiors
Photography by: Paul S. Bartholomew

As an alternative to the traditional library, this room is centered on playing games with family and friends. Bold colors in the fabrics of rich browns, various reds, and warm golds were chosen to add warmth and life to the space. As a focal point, a custom-designed, skirted game table and four comfortable chairs were centered in the room. The windows were dressed with soft Roman shades, using a bold Ikat patterned velvet and each trimmed with a fun wooden bobbin fringe. For a casual look, we covered the floor with an unusual chunky handspun jute carpet. To add some reflection and light, we added gold-toned wallpaper to the ceiling and mirrored the back of the wood bookcases. We removed a section of bookshelves in one area and created a fabric bulletin board where we displayed scorecards and ribbons. We then filled the room with various books, games, and puzzles as well as art and decorative objects.

living

rooms

48

"Perfect Canvas" Living Room
Newport Showhouse Guild, Newport, Rhode Island
Marc Bordet of Bordet Interiors Design

This room was the perfect canvas to create a space with several sitting areas comfortable for conversation and entertaining. I was inspired by the Italian and South of France elegant lifestyle. Comfortable yet elegant furniture makes this room feel welcome. The ceilings and the walls are stenciled with a gold leafing pattern. Given the extent of the intricate work, it took over two months to paint the ceiling and walls.

Living Room: Auburn Valley Home Tour
Auburn Valley Symphony Home Tour, Country Club Elegance
Joyce Hoshall of Joyce Hoshall, Interiors
Photography by: Dave Adams

Open space with architectural details of soaring windows
and twenty-five foot rafters create a loft-like feeling.

Beach Living Room
Cape May's Fifth Annual Designer Show House
Carole Roach of DRD & Associates
Photography by: John Armich

The beach has been brought into the living room with a dune day bed and matching dune arm chairs, dune-inspired area carpets, and shell-colored wall paint.

Elegant, Comfortable Living Room
Princeton Designer Showhouse & Gardens XV
Totten-McGuirl Interiors
Photography by: Paul S. Bartholomew

This elegant and comfortable living room is a space created for yesterday and today. Antiques, art deco furniture, and traditional pieces have been combined with a restrained color palette of aqua and cream to compliment the beautiful neoclassical details of this room.

Elegant, Comfortable Living Room
Princeton Designer Showhouse & Gardens XV
Totten-McGuirl Interiors
Photography by: Paul S. Bartholomew

Horse Farm Living Room/Parlor

Decorators' Showhouse, Corinthia Horse Farm, north of Lexington, Kentucky
Joe T. Richardson, Carolyn Threlkeld, and Bobbie Alloo of Hubbuch & Co.
Photography by: Walt Roycraft

The first floor living room/parlor features an antique
Waterford chandelier, hand gilt folding screens in silver
and gold metallic sheeting, a pair of matching sofas, a pair
of French styled gallery tables, antique Oushak rug, and
period antiques.

Great Room
Napa Valley Symphony League 2010 Home and Garden Tour, Yountville, California, An Italian Style Farmhouse
Joyce Hoshall of Joyce Hoshall, Interiors
Photography by: Dave Adams

The main living space has a play of textures—white plaster walls, dark hand hewn beams, and hickory plank floors. A Knole sofa, zebra ottoman, and Italian leather chairs help complete the comfy textural look.

Lower Level Family Room
Cape May's Fourth Annual Designer Show House
Mark D. Little of Design Home Interiors
Photography by: John Armich

The lower level family room is a retreat from the world above with a sea of sandy neutrals in a modern interpretation of the Craftsman style. Rich, dark woods anchor the geometric patterns and organic taupe hues of the down-filled sectional. Cuddled by elegant sconces projecting warm light, this sanctuary offers comfortable ambience for visiting family and friends. Crisp accents in vibrant green provide a playful environment in which to be entertained with a game of billiards. Surrounded by subtle, patterned comfort and rich, espresso wood tones, ample seating creates the perfect casual, yet elegant, lounge.

sitting gathe

ringkeeping

Parlor
Cape May's Sixth Annual Designer Show House
Mark D. Little of Design Home Interiors
Photography by: John Armich

The past meets the future in this Hollywood glam-inspired parlor. Traditional elements, combined with serene slate blues, soft neutrals, and feminine details surround guests as they take a step into the perfect blend of fantasy and reality. By creating focal points out of structured architectural elements, a transformation occurs within the space that creates a casual and contemporary, yet sophisticated environment with soft metallics, textural fabrics, and luxurious comfort.

His and Her Family Sitting Room and Terrace

2010 DC Design House, Chevy Chase, Maryland
Kelley Proxmire of Kelley Interior Design
Photography by: Lydia Cutter, exterior
Angie Seckinger, interiors

The living room was envisioned as a "His and Her" family sitting room, an elegant retreat where the Mr. and Mrs. can read, write, and relax in comfort and style. The sitting room was designed around a brown and white damask print by Schumacher. Graphic and graceful, the fabric sets the tone for the room's masculine/feminine dynamic. Dark brown walls, punctuated by white drapery and upholstery, and unexpected accents of gray provide a contemplative setting and effect both restful and refreshing.

The exceptional number of windows and doors in the space presented an inherent design challenge. The creative solution anchors the center of the room with a stunning, octagonal table and creates seating vignettes in the corners. The furniture is arranged to accommodate two people comfortably. Desks are tucked into the small space: a vintage writing table positioned for natural light by the window; a second pullout desk cleverly built into the custom cabinetry. Multiple seating areas allow for a cozy read on the sofa, or a chat in the pull up chairs across the room.

The palette of browns, white, and grays continues on the adjoining garden terrace. A gun metal coffee table defines the principal seating area. A fountain and Sargent white flowering crab apple trees in white planters provide emphasis. Accent pillows in a chocolate brown indoor/outdoor fabric feature a dogwood appliqué and complement furnishings upholstered in white matelassé.

Sheer Nostalgia
Mansions & Millionaires® Designers' Showcase® 2008, Mill Neck Manor, Mill Neck, New York
Katharine Posillico McGowan of Katharine Jessica Interior Design, LLC
Photography by: Oleg March

The inspiration for the sitting room started with the wallpaper; its rich sheen creates an elegant backdrop while the bold pattern moves the eye through the many angles of the space. Fabrics were selected that complemented the paper and emphasized the glamorous feeling of the 1920s. The pieces of furniture are a blend of comfort and beauty, combining comfortable upholstery with more delicate case goods and occasional pieces. The goal was to create a glamorous, yet comfortable retreat for a woman to enjoy as her own personal space—to write or dream in her own room or on her private terrace, away from the main areas of the home.

The Jewel Box
Historical Society of Hammonton Designer Showhouse
Mary Jo Gallagher of Greystone Interiors, LLC

A small retreat to read, dream or even enjoy a cup of tea! Special and sweet, soft colors, surrounded by the things you love where the cares of the world are left at the door.

Back Patio
Cape May's Fourth Annual Designer Showhouse
Vera Bahou of Designhaus Interiors
Photography by: John Armich

Time, style, and richness were used to design the wet bar area and luxurious, sensual style to design the cozy, semi-outdoor back patio. Craftsman-style architecture is a reflection of the 1910 era by Otis Townsend. The theme of the wet bar space came about from the collection of ingredients already mentioned—time, style, and richness. It harkens back in time to the arts and crafts period of Frank Lloyd Wright. The shape of the bar represents movement and, combined with the use of natural onyx, is repeated into the space with different applications. The artistic presentations that is seen on the ceiling and walls is especially customized for this room. Lighting design depicts the arts and crafts period and adds sensual illumination of style and color.

Bamboozled
2010 Bucks County Designer House & Gardens
David Fierabend of Groundswell Design Group
Photography by: Katrina Mojzesz of Top Kat Photography Inc.

"Bamboozled" is a 900 square-foot installation creating an outdoor living space that demonstrates how design can transform an ordinary and less-than-ideal spot into a truly magical environment. Starting with the ground level, a few of the existing pavers were removed to create planting spaces. Into these, freshly harvested twelve-foot bamboo poles were sunk into concrete. Around their bases sedums and succulents were planted. Now height connected the ground to the sky, and these verticals also created curvy spaces that made the patio area far more interesting.

Shards of glass and mirrors from the property were used to create free-form mosaics on the back wall, capturing glints of sunlight and animating the space as well as using recycled materials to decorate. To plant the space, we created a living salad garden on a table balanced on a tree trunk. Between the growing elements of lettuces, tomatoes, squash, and cucumbers, a table was set for a meal, with plates and cutlery.

We like combining practical and fantasy elements in the design, such as our treehouse, which girdles an existing tree without damaging it. You ascend to the treehouse via a bamboo and rope ladder, and the platform provides a viewing station for the garden that helps you see it in a new way, a miniature world with a farm element and a human element—harmonious living.

Side Porch

The Hampton Designer Showhouse, Sag Harbor, Long Island, New York
Annemarie DiSalvo and Keith Mazzei of diSalvo Interiors
Photography by: Michael J. Rodenbush

When a space is designed, the principle of function and purpose of the space dictates the direction. However, the designers decided from the outset that they were going to approach the design as a multi-functional outdoor room with a South Beach vibe, defining several dedicated functions inspired by the landscape areas and the large private pool. Thinking outside of the box, the designers created an outdoor shower with a fabric canopy, and weathered bamboo stalks that were used as privacy walls.

K

hens

Farm Kitchen
Napa Valley Symphony League 2010 Home and Garden Tour, Yountville, California, An Italian Style Farmhouse
Joyce Hoshall of Joyce Hoshall, Interiors
Photography by: Dave Adams

Twenty-first century farmhouse kitchen, with exposed beams, irridescent mosaic backsplash, and red knobed Wolf 6 burner range.

Glamorous Grey Kitchen
Design Show House at the Winter Cottage, Caumsett, Lloyd Neck, Long Island, New York
Laurie Duke of Studio Guiliana Designs
Photography by: Ivy D

Inspired by this beautiful home's glorious and architecturally relevant past, I was excited by the challenge to make it sparkle once again. When designing the space, I carefully selected materials and finishes reflective of the home's distinguished roots. I imagined the patina and sparkle of a fine piece of jewelry, which had been handed down through generations. A beautiful, calming palette of grey, white, silver, gold, and a combination of textures return the room to its elegant beginnings, similar to a loved piece of jewelry.

All the moldings and trim details currently in place were added, since the room had been void of any of these details. Recessed panels were built into the deep-set windows, as were the solid wood casings surrounding the window openings. They were all inspired by the attention to details found throughout the rest of the house. Newly built raised panel cabinets and pilasters flank the sink. The cabinetry reflects the period in which architect John Russell Pope Marble designed the home.

A combination of carefully chosen antiques and collectables are combined with clean modern shapes to keep the room fresh and welcoming. These objects may have been collected through the years had this kitchen remained in operation. Many are displayed in a floor to ceiling built in plate rack, which I envisioned to look as if it had always been there. As with any well-designed room, this is a balance of a combination of architectural details, polished and matte finishes, along with a refined color palette. Beginning with the custom silk and antique lace valances, to the domino sugar boxes displayed in the cabinetry, a sunny yellow accent color adds just the right amount of pop to an otherwise neutral palette.

Quaint Quarters: A Cottage Kitchen
Mansions in May Designer Show House, 2012, Fawn Hill Farm, Morristown, New Jersey
Morgan House Interiors
Photography by: Paul Bartholomew

The kitchen in the cottage is a quaint space designed for the grandmother of the family. The space is updated with new cabinets, countertops, and appliances, but still embodies the qualities of a country farm home. The butter cream colored custom cabinets warm the space and are a nice contrast against the brick floor. Open shelves, decorative legs, and chicken wire/glass cabinets lend a soft feel to the modernized appliances.

The pantry is converted into a craft room, with all the craft supplies to keep Grandma busy. The rest of the pantry is used as overflow storage from the kitchen. Cabinetry and shelving is smartly designed and offers an aesthetically organized look.

Although the space is small, which is always a challenge, it contains compact, modernized appliances and offers all the amenities of a large kitchen on a smaller scale.

Breakfast Room

Old Westbury Gardens: Home for the Holidays, Old Westbury, Long Island, New York
Rosemarie diSalvo of diSalvo Interiors
Photography by: Steve Geraci—Reflex Photo

The theme was "Christmas Breakfast at Tiffany's." Tiffany & Co. provided all of the props, including different size gift boxes and allowed us to use their signature color on the wall. Designing the Breakfast Room was an opportunity to create our vision of a glamourous setting. Tiffany's signature gift boxes were stacked and positioned to create a unique table scape dripping with pearls. Glass "diamond-shaped" beads were scattered on the table as a backdrop to the silk table cloth. Beautiful, oversized black and white photos of scenes from the iconic movie provided by Accetra Arts, Ltd. framed the walls. The room was like stepping into a Tiffany's jewel box.

dining

rooms

Holiday Dining Room
Holidays Decorators Show House, Newport, Rhode Island
Marc Bordet of Bordet Interiors Design

I was asked to design a holidays table setting in one of the magnificent rooms of the Newport Museum of Fine Arts using the art as a background. The antique furniture belongs to the museum estate.

Shady Side Dining Room
Shady Side, Paris Pike, Lexington, Kentucky
Joe T. Richardson, Carolyn Threlkeld, and Bobbie Alloo of Hubbuch & Co.
Photography by: Walt Roycraft

Shady Side is an antebellum house built in 1792 on Paris Pike in Lexington, Kentucky. The design takes its inspiration from the hand-blocked Zuber wallcovering executed in the classic pattern "El Durado," which was first printed in the 1840s. The dining table featured European china and crystal with table top accents in Lalique glassware, underscored with an antique Serapi rug.

Whimsical, Colorful Dining Room
Stamford Designer Showhouse, 2010, Stamford, Connecticut
Kenneth/Davis

The dining room design allowed us to create a room with a whimsical and colorful feel. The room lacquered in a bright blue added the punch of color and the backdrop for the distinguished pieces. Pulling from the past, we lacquered Chippendale chairs white and upholstered them in a white crocodile. The dining table was skirted using a blue and white delph pattern fabric, which was also brought up to the window. The table and chairs rest on an orange and blue area rug with an octagonal link pattern. This pattern was brought up to the ceiling. Over top of the dining table hangs a free form contemporary orchid chandelier, which moves to the breeze. The artwork, done on Lucite, added the next dimension to finish off the room.

"The Man Who Came to Dinner"
43rd Pasadena Showcase House of Design
Gregory Parker of Parker West Interiors
Photography by: Alexander Vertikoff

This dining room reflects the strong interest in Chinese and Japanese style that was a part of the history of this house. A bubinga rosewood table on a bronze base is centered in the room. This table top is a solid piece of wood from a tree that fell naturally in the forest. It is over 600 years old. I love the idea of mixing natural organic forms with formal traditions, be it Eastern or Western traditional furniture. This allows furniture to be viewed as art. The natural, organic forms remind us of the origin of our materials. Flanking each end of the table are antique Ming armchairs accompanied by six sleek modern armchairs. A 12' x 16' wool and silk rug with an interlocking ring design anchors the table in the center of the room. Above the table is a custom "Cloud" chandelier of hand blown glass. Hanging in front of the large mirror is a custom-carved Chinese screen with decorative accents. This layering effect is also a juxtaposing of Eastern and Western design traditions. This eclectic approach is at the core of my design aesthetic. Floors are stained a dark walnut. The wall finish reflects the color of parchment. In the picture window area, the small oval table with two chairs creates the perfect vignette and serves as a dessert table if needed. Flexibility in space and a heightened sense of function inform my work.

Traditional and Modern Dining Room
Design Show House at the Winter Cottage, Caumsett, Lloyd Neck, Long Island, New York
Claudia Dowling of Claudia Dowling Interiors
Photography by: Ivy D

Utilizing a mixture of traditional and modern interior design components, the intent was to capture twenty-first century living in a way that rejuvenates, inspires, and encompasses the essence of living well. Louis XVI dining room chairs are a nice complement to the Asian-influenced contemporary demi-lune console. The Asian motif is repeated in the ethereal theme of the wallpaper. Over the fireplace is a custom painting by Daniel Del Orfano, created especially for the area. The entire room provides a harmonious setting to enjoy a glass of wine and delectable meal with friends and family.

Italian Farmhouse Dining Room

Napa Valley Symphony League 2010 Home and Garden Tour, Yountville, California, An Italian Style Farmhouse
Joyce Hoshall of Joyce Hoshall, Interiors
Photography by: Dave Adams

Italian farmhouse style dining—a juxtapostion of elements including a table with a reclaimed wood top from old railroad cars and iron legs, surrounded by sumptuous, classical "Ebinasta" upholstered chairs.

Headley-Whitney Dining Room
Decorator Showcase, Headley-Whitney House
Joe T. Richardson, Carolyn Threlkeld, and Bobbie Alloo of Hubbuch & Co.
Photography by: Walt Roycraft

The dining room features a hand-painted sepia wall mural, Baccarat chandelier, and hand-painted Anna Weatherly china. Furnishings include a George III demi-lune sideboard, a George II walnut gilt mirror c. 1745, and a George III cabinet/bookcase c. 1800, from a Southern estate.

bedr

ooms

Octopus Garden Bedroom
Cape May's Fourth Annual Designer Show House
Betsy King of Jupiter Dunes Designs
Photography by: John Armich

This bedroom is in the very back of the house called the "Carpenter Cottage" in Victorian Cape May, New Jersey. The house was to return to its owners at the close of the season. The bedroom I designed will be occupied by the young, contemporary adult daughter of the owners. She is a hard-working marine biologist who spends months at sea studying squid and plankton. I wanted to create a relaxing space in a traditional seashore color scheme, but with a more contemporary feel. The bed is nestled between two natural wood built-in closets and faces a large, open wall. I designed an undersea mural that covered the complete wall. It was artfully executed by Mary Dima of Daroo Designs. Sea-green and aqua waterscape walls reflect hazy, muted visions of ocean life that envelope the room. In a hideaway beneath the waves, copper and gold accents and touches of translucent glass reflect the morning sun. Oversized custom mosaic wall sconces by Luna Bella Lighting cast prism reflections across the room. I have designed and fabricated gently twisting patina copper vines to surround the recessed sleeping area of rich textured fabrics and fluffy pillows—all giving a feeling of "The Octopus' Garden in the Shade."

Bedroom: Slumber Party for Teens
Auburn Valley Symphony Home Tour, Country Club Elegance
Joyce Hoshall of Joyce Hoshall, Interiors
Photography by: Dave Adams

The four-poster beds give a sense of enclosure to the teenagers—forgetting all about their sleeping bags.

Bedroom
Symphony Guild of Charlotte's Designer House at the Met Terraces at Metropolitan, Charlotte, North Carolina
Betty F. Kohn of Marlboro Interiors
Photography by: Dustin Peck

"With new construction one needs to introduce a sense of history. What better way than to pair collected treasures with present-day comfort!"

A hand-carved gold leaf mirror hangs above a hand-painted vintage piece with a crystal vase, lamp, and books. A large shell echoes the wall color. The mirror reflects the desk by the window. An antique Dutch painting of a lady hangs above the desk while an antique mahogany chest, circa 1870, with slender lamps, quill box, and Staffordshire figures are placed opposite the bed. Hanging above the chest are engraved prints of Henry the Eighth's court by the Italian artist Bartolozzi.

Seashore Living, Second Floor Bedroom
Cape May Annual Designer Show House 2009 – Franklin Street
Mary Jane Soens of MJ Designs
Photography by: Mary Jane Soens & John Armich

Our ancestors brought their treasures from the past and added new items as needed, making their homes an eclectic collection of old and new. We re-used a headboard and added a new chest of drawers, nightstand, and rocker. Adding new window treatments and bedding to the room created an inviting and comfortable guest room.

The soft colors of the sea, sand, and local greenery were found in the paint, fabrics, and furniture. Representing life in Cape May County were accents of metal on the window treatments, including grommets, dock line, and cleats to represent the fishing and boating industries. Two fabrics were used, both in soft hues of oyster and oatmeal. A lined Roman shade and two dead hung panels of a material created to look like fishing nets were used to frame the window. Fabrics included colors of blue, beige, soft yellows, and greens with images of palm trees, pineapples, and seashells representing the beach environment. Mindful of the use of products from production to end use, Indoor-Outdoor fabric was chosen for the top bed, to help prevent mold and mildew from wet towels and bathing suits. The chest of drawers and night stand were stained to complement the existing woodwork. Large scale photographic images on canvas of body boarders and surfers added to today's fun at the beach. A rocking chair so often seen on our porches completed the look, in a turquoise blue with matching seat cushions using the fabric from the window's Roman shade.

Caumsett Bedroom

Caumsett Showhouse, Lloyd Neck, Long Island, New York
Judith Lattuca of Judith Designs
Photography by: Ivy D

A famous fashion model has come to spend the weekend. Lawn parties, yachting, and Black Tie Balls are on the agenda. Glamour and fame are her game, and she is feeling right at home in these luxurious surroundings.

Breezy, fresh, and glamorous, this bedroom is classic and modern at the same time. The designer chose a cool palette of soft water blue and white, which was inspired by the water view from the window and the light that infuses the room. The light blue color is complemented by shiny silver finishes and flourishes, and accented with ebony touches.

When you enter the bedroom, you will immediately notice the custom bed, which is adorned with fine luxury linens that invite you to slumber or languish in their softness. The two windows are treated with elegant custom draperies fabricated from two different silk fabrics. They hang from black metal hardware chosen by the designer to balance the ebony accents in the room.

Guest Bedroom

Cape May Annual Designer Show House
Mary Jo Gallagher of Greystone Interiors, LLC
Photography by: John Armich

The original, dark craftsman-style woodwork and the warm, classic colors combine to give guests a cozy relaxing retreat, where they can unwind and feel at home. It will surely influence them to visit more often!

Guest Bedroom: Green for Serene
Auburn Valley Symphony Home Tour, Country Club Elegance
Joyce Hoshall of Joyce Hoshall, Interiors
Photography by: Dave Adams

The room invites you to enjoy the freshness of the green and white color pallet while opening to the golf course beyond.

Guest Bedroom
Napa Valley Symphony League 2010 Home and Garden Tour, Yountville, California, An Italian Style Farmhouse
Joyce Hoshall of Joyce Hoshall, Interiors
Photography by: Dave Adams

Guest bedroom with circa 1800 twin beds and Italian secretary.

Office/Guest Combination
Auburn Valley Symphony Home Tour, Country Club Elegance
Joyce Hoshall of Joyce Hoshall, Interiors
Photography by: Dave Adams

Sundrenched office and guest combination is highlighted with an antique iron daybed, which beckons to rest awhile or just write a note while enjoying the view.

bathr

ooms

Master Bath
Napa Valley Symphony League 2010 Home and Garden Tour, Yountville, California, An Italian Style Farmhouse
Joyce Hoshall of Joyce Hoshall, Interiors
Photography by: Dave Adams

Italian Calacutta honed marble, exposed beam master bath
with contemporary stainless faucetry.

Exotic Moroccan Influence Fantasy
Cape May's Fourth Annual Designer Showhouse, Cape May, New Jersey
Lorraine Byrne of Michael Byrne Painting, Inc.
Photography by: John Armich

The exotic Moroccan influence fantasy second floor bathroom was executed in less than two weeks, on a small budget and little time. This bathroom is an interpretation of the Morris tradition of a medieval or esoteric theme in the Arts and Craft movement. Enter into the mysterious ambiance, where luxurious, sparkling beaded trim and embroidered fabric sets the scene for a dramatic seating area. A Middle Eastern feel continues with a ceiling-draped rice paper canopy, and encompasses an exotic carved wood bench with satin sea blue seat cushion, layered with comfortable beaded and trimmed patterned pillows in colors of blues, rusts, and golds. The seating area is filled with standing and hanging medieval candle holders. On the wall is a framed watercolor of *A Moroccan Woman*. The aroma of sandalwood envelopes you as you move forward to the focal point … a surprise show area featuring a reflective mosaic design in a Sicus Tile …1" x 1" glass iridescent tile expertly crafted and centered with an estate metal centerpiece. Sea glass 4" x 4" tiles of blues and greens in the corner of the design, as well as in the tub, along with dark iron and wood with folded embellished towels in jewel tones, create the mood. The wall color of rasha gold and baha red on the textured, painted swirled ceiling, adds richness and glow with light reflecting patterns.

Upstairs Bathroom

RNS Showhouse **at the Shore**—Windsong on Wesley, Ocean City, New Jersey
Mary Jo Gallagher of Greystone Interiors, LLC
Photography by: Antonimages.com

Inspired by the craftsman-style architecture of this 1907 house, each detail was carefully selected to echo the past and yet still remain timeless, clean, and fresh. Hand-painted maritime flags carry a special message.

First Floor Powder Room
Cape May's Fourth Annual Designer Show House, Otis Townsend Residence
Carole Roach of DRD & Associates
Photography by: John Armich

In the first floor powder room, a suitcase of the 1915 era coordinates with the Frank Lloyd Wright-inspired faux stained glass window overlay. A teak stool represents the furniture utilized on the decks of grand old cruise liners of that time. A hint of Victorian carry-over is included in this room. You can envision a world traveler wanting to take respite in this colorful beach home powder room.

Guest Bathroom
Napa Valley Symphony League 2010 Home and Garden Tour, Yountville, California, An Italian Style Farmhouse
Joyce Hoshall of Joyce Hoshall, Interiors
Photography by: Dave Adams

Limestone walled powder bath with 800 pound carrera marble sink creates tension with sparkly crystal lighting.

Dorothy Parker

2009 Designer House & Gardens in Bucks County, Pennsylvania
Tom Gass of Gass Design
Photography by: Katrina Mojzesz of Top Kat Photography inc.

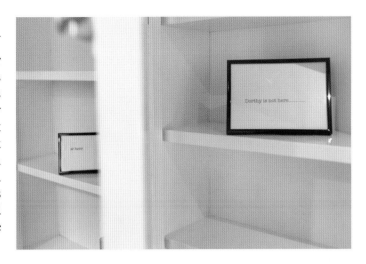

There was a great forty's style in the black and white floor and the over-scaled pedestal sink. What came to mind was the great humorist and critic, Dorothy Parker, of Bucks County. In that venue, black and white portraits of Dorothy by Gass, with her famous quotes, grace the new, lustrous, soft green Venetian plaster walls. A self-glowing ceiling track with pin spots on the portraits, with hanging hand-blown bubble globe pendants, reflect in a Deco style mirror. A crisp white Roman shade, robe, and towels with Dorothy's monogram personalize the space. Steno pad, cigarettes, and a stack of *Vanity Fair* magazines complete this playful tribute to one of Bucks County's great legends.

specialpur

posespaces

Casita

Napa Valley Symphony League 2010 Home and Garden Tour, Yountville, California, An Italian Style Farmhouse
Joyce Hoshall of Joyce Hoshall, Interiors
Photography by: Dave Adams

Separate from the main house, an enticing *casita* beckons.
The *Casita* bedroom features a citrus green poster bed.

Aperitif

Mansions & Millionaires® Designers' Showcase® 2009, La Selva, Upper Brookville, New York
Katharine Posillico McGowan of Katharine Jessica Interior Design, LLC
Photography by: Keith Scott Morton

The inspiration for the solarium began with the color violet; in 2009 this color was very important in fashion and design. Violet combines the stability of blue with the energy of red and symbolizes luxury, ambition, and extravagance. I wanted the room to be elegant but at the same time have a casual comfort. I achieved this by selecting furnishings that had very sophisticated, flowing lines, but are fairly simple and comfortable. The muted violet fabrics convey an airy, open, warm feeling that is perfect for a sun-filled solarium.

The goal was to have a glamorous, yet comfortable room to enjoy cocktails with friends or read a book and bask in the light of the large windows and French doors. The name Aperitif signifies the concept of the use of the space. Mixtures of textures in fabrics and furnishings give the room a unique feeling.

Sanctuary

2009 Designer Showhouse & Gardens in Bucks County, Pennsylvania
Lisa Cicalese McMillen of Cica Lisa Designs
Photography by: Katrina Mojzesz of Top Kat Photography Inc.

The concept of the room was a private, glamorous, organized creative space that could be a sanctuary or command center for the woman of the house. I surveyed a few dozen women, took suggestions from female visitors to the Empty House party, and added my own desires. Taking the room from concept to reality required, first, defining the exact functionality of the space. Furniture pieces and placement set the room in motion. Color came next. I knew I wanted to divide the space with color, use a metallic palette, and glass beads. To keep the soft palette from looking too sweet and young, black was added in the rug and trim. Adding silver leaf to a vintage secretary brings a piece with beautiful lines into a new century, but retains its sophistication. Still looking for a chair, I happened upon the turquoise tufted chair. It added an unexpected pop of color, which made the whole room come alive!

 I added a bit of myself to the room by creating collages drawing from my fashion design background. I think they really finish the room.

"Ancient Paths:" Adult Rumpus Room

2011 San Francisco Decorator Showcase
Philpotts Interiors
Photography by: Matthew Millman

Designing a showhouse is not always what it seems. The design, while liberating, is the designers own private interpretation of a space. Three Honolulu interior designers combined their talents to create this show-stopping room in style savvy San Francisco. The budget, cost, and overhead, however, are also the designer's. Something's borrowed and something's blue? Well, sort of. Their challenge was to take a space that no one wanted and make it engaging, using a fresh approach. In other words, their intent was not to decorate, but to create a space that was experiential, not simply filled with "fluff and stuff."

They took a bowling alley of a space with a drop-dead bay view and turned it into an "adult rumpus room" by creating a gallery to a tribal tune. The metamorphosis was done with the sophisticated use of color and tribal patterns. The resulting international vibe gives permission to view the room's digital photography with a background of primitive music.

As the sun set across San Francisco Bay, the room came alive with the deep navy walls receding and the dramatic, large scale photographs coming to the forefront, punctuated by primal video and audio. The room pulsed and enlivened all the senses.

The playful lighting throws primitive patterns on the floor, creating just the right graphic tension. Furniture, rugs, and artful accent lights anchor the seating groups. The art is lit with color-connected LED track lights. Three deco lights create distinct zones.

This room expands the definition of a gallery, making it more relevant to the way we live and play, less uptight and more authentic. It's all about the experience of letting go.

"Think Big" Master Dressing Room and Rotunda
The 2010 Designer Showhouse of New Jersey, Saddle River, New Jersey
Valerie Onor Interior Design
Photography by: Phillip Ennis

Inspiration sprung from the adage that "good things do come in small packages." The Rotunda is a hub, a connector and a transitional space for the Master Suite and the Dressing Room. Valerie grounded the hub with a central table, the perfect repository for a purse or vase, and chose a color that would center the space with just a whisper of what lay beyond in the neighboring Master Dressing Room. She designed the space to be inviting, yet functional, outfitting it with all the seating, storage, and lighting that one needs either to get ready in a rush or luxuriate in privacy. A colorful mix of warm pink, raspberry, green, aubergine, and a touch of gold refreshes the spirit and brightens each day.

Bit and Bridle Tack Room
2010 Bucks County Designer House, Bucks County, Pennsylvania
Kevin McPheeters of Chapel Road Design, LLC
Photography by: John Armich

The tack room had a softer feel more appropriate for the contemplation of the post-hunt tasks: overstuffed chairs and a gilt table juxtaposed the tack area where saddles and bridles hang upon the walls. A variety of textures and accessories were featured throughout, a realistically wood grained vinyl floor overlaid with sisal and hide rugs, linen, pine, leather, the glint of metals, and stone.

The key was to be able to enjoy the horse theme, yet also appeal universally to an audience less familiar with the workings of the stable. A fantasy of the wild hunt and sophisticated etiquette in the designer's interpretation of the world equine.

master

suites

Globe-Trotting Bachelor Pad

Hampton Designer Showhouse 2009, Bridgehampton, New York
Benjamin Bradley and David Thiergartner of Bradley Thiergartner Interiors Inc.
Photography by: Phillip Ennis

Bradley Thiergartner's fictitious client was a single, well-traveled man whose interests lie in art, literature, music, and collecting. The primary focus in the room was given to a custom designed "Knoll" bed done in classic black and white cotton ticking. Mahogany finials, crisp linen sheets, a leopard pillow, and a classic Hermes throw all allude to the worldliness of the inhabitant. A Giacometti-inspired writing desk from Carol Gratale serves as a nightstand on the right side of the bed and a large antique mahogany game table serves the left side. Two chairs created by French artist Christian Augustivielle for Holly Hunt punctuate the room and further add to the eclectic mix.

In the far corner of the room, his own (unfinished) artwork, and a burled Yew wood plant stand from Ann Morris Antiques and custom quilted linen curtains complete that elevation.

The art collection and objets d'arte together with the choice of materials both sooths the eye and invigorates the soul at the same time.

A Place for Grace: Master Suite
Mansion in May Designer Show House, 2010, Fawn Hill Farm Estate, Morristown, New Jersey
Karla Trincanello of Interior Decisions, Inc.

The room was inspired by Grace Kelly, the Princess of Monaco, as a tribute in the year she would have been eighty years old. A master suite in the show house was designed as an American summer retreat for the Princess to use as a home base while visiting her family in Philadelphia, New Jersey, and New York. American art and Hollywood glamour are found throughout the space designed for an American-born princess who might have wished for private and comfortable luxury different from the Rococo Palace in Monaco.

The Master Bedroom
Mansion in May Designer Show House, 2008
Kenneth/Davis

As one enters this suite, one is invited to jump into the custom-painted four poster queen size canopy bed in Strong White, which will be made up with luxurious bed linens in Egyptian cotton and silk. The ceiling of the canopy is in a raised panel design. Flanking the canopy bed is a pair of Chinese-inspired chests, also lacquered in white, with lamps resembling Foo dogs resting on them. The window treatments are solid silk side panels on chrome and glass rods, which puddle on the floor. At the foot of the bed are a pair of chrome benches in a triangular design, which are covered in a lime green and white patterned fabric. Once in the bed, one can view a favorite movie in the Mediterranean inspired armoire, which has been lacquered in Strong White.

St. Regis Master Bedroom

2009 Atlanta Symphony Associates Decorators' Show House
Patricia McLean Interiors, Inc.
Photography by: Jake Laughlin; Lauren Rubinstein; and Erica Dines

The room measures 22' x 30'. Panels bring the scale down. It features custom milled woodwork, chair rail, and panels. The marble mantle was brought in by the designer and added to an existing wall purely for aesthetics. Three areas include the Sitting Room, Breakfast Table (St. Regis concierge service for residents displayed), and the Bedroom. English, Italian and French antique furniture and paintings enhance the setting. The chandeliers and lighting were imported from England.

Photographer: Jake Laughlin

Photographer: Jake Laughlin

Photographer: Lauren Rubinstein

Photographer: Lauren Rubinstein

Photographer: Erica Dines

Le Dolce Vita: Master Bedroom
2010 Atlanta Symphony Associates Decorators' Show House, Atlanta, Georgia
Patricia McLean Interiors, Inc.
Photography by: Patricia McLean; Lauren Rubinstein

A Venetian inspired theme was chosen for the master bedroom. The dramatic oil painting of Venice over the mantle sets the tone and the color palate for the room. The duchesse brisee and the fireside chair are covered in elegant velvets for a rich Italian feel. The sunburst on the firescreen underscores the European feel.

Photographer: Lauren Rubinstein

My Suite Embraceable You

Mansions & Millionaires® Designers' Showcase® 2009, La Selva Mansion in Mill Neck, Long Island, New York
Valerie Onor Interior Design
Photography by: Keith Scott Morton

Great style, like great music and great love, never goes out of fashion. This three bedroom suite is homage to an era of elegance and romance. This significant, second floor space was designed with great care, creating an ultra-romantic bedroom that nods to the past while remaining firmly based in the present. The inspiration was the commanding mural in the bed alcove featuring a Chinese pavilion, mountains, and exotic birds original to the home's 1915 décor. The technique used is called "marouflage," a 3,000-year-old technique whereby artists' adhesives were applied to both the wall and the canvas before adding paint. Coordinated panels were artfully designed to extend the mural, while still leaving the original panel as a focal point. Onor's workroom painstakingly replicated the mural in the two added end panels, gradually reducing the intensity of their color moving outward to seamlessly blend with the soft palette of the room—hues of aqua, ochre, and green.

The room is replete with lush furnishings—velvets, silks, a touch of lace, and soft colors that lend warmth and enhance the romantic mood. The modern and sophisticated audio visual system is integrated invisibly into the room—notably within the nineteenth century rosewood cabinet that houses the retractable flat-screen TV. The connecting bathroom and dressing room are adjoining. The bath, carefully refurbished and preserved, maintains its vintage quality. Original brass fixtures, antique wall scale, and tile coexist comfortably with new amenities—fresh wallpaper, fine linens, and accessories. Her dressing room continues to augment the room's plush feeling with a pair of feminine fireside chairs, hand-painted chest of drawers, and retro dressing table and tufted, upholstered seat.

Sweet Suite Serenity
2008 DC Design House, Georgetown, Washington, DC
Kelley Proxmire of Kelley Interior Design
Photography by: Angie Seckinger

This master bedroom is a luxurious retreat from the outside world. A serene, two-toned palette of pale aqua and cream envelops the room. The scheme centers around a large-scale medallion print from Brunschwig & Fils, which frames the bed as a dramatic floor-to-ceiling draping and continues as accents throughout the room. While the color scheme is uncomplicated, rich textures introduce a sense of luxury. Windows are swathed in layer upon layer of creamy silk. Touches of antique gold add sophistication to the painted furniture. A sleek acrylic vanity table gives an edge to classic elegance.

Master Suite
American Fashion-Designers at the Aldyn, New York, New York
James Rixner of James Rixner, Inc.
Photography by: Nick Johnson

An elegant master bedroom suite inspired by the rich palette and beautiful detailing of Josie Natori's snow lion series. The snow lion is the celestial emblem of Tibet and represents a mind and body that are in complete harmony.

The warm fall colors of saffron, curry, and olive evoke a sense of serenity. Venetian plastered walls serve as the perfect backdrop for a unique blend of color, texture, and sophisticated furniture selection.

Since bedrooms are most often seen as the inner sanctum of the home, this one invites you in to relax and reflect, enabling one to transcend to a more peaceful state.

Master Sitting Room and Master Bedroom
Auburn Valley Symphony Home Tour, Country Club Elegance
Joyce Hoshall of Joyce Hoshall, Interiors
Photography by: Dave Adams

The master sitting room and master bedroom were designed with varying values of dove gray, creme, and white, allowing the mind to rest at day's end.

Master Bedroom
Napa Valley Symphony League 2010 Home and Garden Tour
Joyce Hoshall of Joyce Hoshall, Interiors
Photography by: Dave Adams

Master bedroom with contemporary fireplace, exposed beams, showing a play of black and white textiles.

La Selva Bedroom

Mansions & Millionaires® Designers' Showcase®, La Selva Showhouse, Upper Brookville, Long Island, New York
Judith Lattuca of Judith Designs
Photography by: Keith Scott Morton

The designer's inspiration for this bedroom came from the beautiful hand-printed wallpaper made in France. This contemporary adaptation of the classic rose, cascading down the wall, hovers above the French *Directoire* Daybed to create a dramatic feature wall. The colors of the room, which are slate blues, navy, charcoal, and ivory, are strong and dramatic, yet the room is feminine and has a serene quality that is comforting. It reflects the energy of today's woman ... feminine but strong.

As your eye moves around the room, you will notice the window treatment. A grand upholstered cornice and drapery dress the window. White linen is embellished with beautiful banding and trims, and the window seat is upholstered in lush dark slate blue velvet.

An Italian antique mirror secretary and French chair grace the opposite wall, providing a space to sit and write. A soft ivory area rug of wool and silk grounds the room, and classic sketches by Picasso and Matisse accent the walls of this feminine-inspired bedroom.

Lighting for the room is provided by a stunning Gothic Lantern in the center of the room, a rock crystal table lamp in the shape of a gemstone, which sits upon a beautiful round ivory lacquered end table, and a floor lamp with a twisted metal base finished in soft gold.